AF873874

BEGINNER'S GUIDE TO DEBT RECOVERY

COPYRIGHT

First published in Great Britain in 2021 under license to Jestina Media Limited

Registered office 78 York Street, London W1H 1DP

Copyright © 2021 by Jestina Limited

All Rights Reserved. No part of this publication may be reproduced, stored in, or introduced into a retrieval system, or transmitted in any form, or by any means (electronic, mechanical, photocopying, recording or otherwise) without the prior permission of the publisher.

The right of Peter John Murray to be identified as the author of the work has been asserted by him in accordance with the Copyright, Designs and Patents Act 1988.

This book is sold subject to the condition that it shall not, by ways of trade or otherwise, be lent, resold, hired out, or otherwise circulated without the publisher's prior consent in any form of binding cover other than that in which it is published, and without a similar condition including this condition being imposed on the subsequent purchaser.

Publisher: Jestina Media Limited

ISBN: 978-1-8382617-0-2

Author: Peter Murray

Writer: Orantes Moore
orantesmoore@gmail.com

Editor: Akosua Annobil
aannobil@gmail.com

Creatives: Lasoke Creative Solutions

Layout and Print: CPUK Print Publishing
www.cp-uk.co.uk

CONTENTS

- Prologue 7
- Debt Recovery and Debt Assignment 11
- Issuing County Court Claims & CCJs 17
- Serving a Statutory Demand 23
- How to Make a Person Bankrupt 25
- Winding-up Petitions 27
- Company Voluntary Arrangement (CVA) 31
- Creditors' Voluntary Liquidation (CVL) 37
- Compulsory Liquidation 43
- Creditors' Guide to Administration 47
- Creditors' Meetings 53
- Making a Misfeasance Claim 57
- Bringing a Professional Negligence Claim 65
- Litigation Funding 69
- Moratorium 73
- Epilogue 77

PROLOGUE

This book was written in 2020, in the midst of the Covid-19 pandemic. The UK government responded to this exceptional crisis by drafting radical new legislation to provide a lifeline for struggling businesses. The Corporate Insolvency and Governance Act was hurriedly enacted in June 2020, introducing temporary and permanent changes to the laws relating to companies and insolvency.

Included in these sweeping amendments were a raft of controversial measures that aimed to:

- Curb company collapses
- Stabilise the UK economy
- Hinder suppliers and creditors in their attempts to collect overdue payments
- Offer insolvent companies and their director(s) considerable protection and time to restructure.

Although the full repercussions and impact of the Act are yet to be determined, it is difficult to fathom how prohibiting creditors from engaging in standard debt enforcement procedures can result in anything but dire consequences.

In some ways the Act is too debtor-friendly, as its measures can easily be abused by a rogue company director who deliberately takes in as many supplies as possible knowing that creditors are unlikely to receive everything they are owed.

For example, the Corporate Insolvency and Governance Act 2020:

- Temporarily suspended the filing of statutory demands and winding-up petitions for Covid-19-related debts (effective until 31 March 2021 at the time of writing)
- Temporarily forbids many medium-sized and large suppliers and creditors from using termination clauses either to stop supply or to ask for additional payments while a company is in a statutory insolvency procedure
- Introduced a moratorium facility that provides companies with protection from creditors and a two-month window to develop a rescue plan
- Provided some company directors with immunity from prosecution for wrongful trading between 1 March 2020 and 30 September 2020.

The government's decision to suspend the filing of statutory demands and winding-up petitions for Covid-19-related debts is a devastating blow for creditors seeking to collect payment of outstanding invoices. While this strategy provides temporary protection for struggling businesses, debt enforcement and insolvency proceedings are essential to the UK economy and restricting their creditors' access to them could prove to be counter-productive in the long term.

To succeed with a winding-up petition, the petitioner must prove the company remains insolvent and was doomed to fail irrespective of Covid-19 (which is only practical for debts incurred in 2019 and some exceptional circumstances).

Another controversial provision of the Corporate Insolvency and Governance Act temporarily suspends the use of termination clauses for many medium-sized and large companies. This section of the legislation prevents suppliers and creditors from using terms and conditions in their contracts either to ask for additional payments or to stop supply of 'essential' goods and services to a company in a statutory insolvency procedure.

However, affected suppliers and creditors have a valid defence to help avoid the suspension if they are able to respond by saying: *'Because of Covid-19, I don't have the resources to purchase the materials I need to supply you as normal.'*

To avoid becoming the victim of a devious company director who abuses this provision, suppliers and creditors should update their terms and conditions to include the following declaration, which must be signed by all new customers:

'I declare that by placing this order and taking your supplies at [insert time] on [insert date], neither I [insert name and job title] nor the company I represent [insert company name] are in any way affected by Covid-19 and have no reason to suspect the coronavirus will in any way influence our previously agreed payment terms.'

Creditors with this provision included in their contracts should have no problem collecting payment as the company will have already confirmed being unaffected by Covid-19 when they took possession of your goods or service. And if your customer is not prepared to make that declaration, why would you want to trade with them?

As the director of multi-award-winning consultancy firm Insolvency & Law, I have spent more than 10 years providing countless numbers of creditors with support, guidance and advice. During that time, I have found that irrespective of your profession or job title, personal and corporate insolvency play a huge role in modern life; they are virtually impossible to avoid.

As a result, this book is dedicated to helping the perplexed creditors I speak with daily who want to educate themselves and learn how to affect and control the course of insolvency proceedings.

DEBT RECOVERY AND DEBT ASSIGNMENT

Debt Recovery

Buyer-supplier relationships are integral in business. In most cases, buyers become debtors by taking goods and services from their suppliers who eventually become creditors. Debt recovery takes place when a third party works on behalf of a supplier/creditor to collect outstanding amounts from a buyer/debtor.

Debt litigation is often expensive and protracted and a creditor's efforts can be easily undermined or derailed by a debtor claiming to have a dispute. After considering the potential for financial loss, most creditors tend to shy away from debt litigation because they know that if things go wrong their costs will escalate, especially if they issued a winding-up petition without first seeking approval from the courts.

How Does Credit Become Debt?

Irrespective of what a supplier sells, they will always prefer to receive payment in advance or upon delivery. But in reality, few can survive operating exclusively on pro-forma payment terms as they will eventually lose business to competitors offering credit. As a result, suppliers are sometimes forced to offer goods and services on credit, usually with terms ranging from seven to 120 days.

An average credit term lasts around 30 days. Debt is considered 'current' during this period, 'aged' once it's overdue and 'bad' after 120 days. Although creditors generally turn a blind eye to late payments, they are legally entitled to engage in enforcement action once the due date has passed and the debt remains unpaid.

Provisions for Disputes

Somewhere on their invoices, orders, delivery notes and website all suppliers should display their sales terms and conditions (also known as terms of engagement, terms of supply, terms of business, sale of contract and sale conditions). Just as it is good business practice and housekeeping to get customers to sign these documents, it is also essential these terms include a provision for disputes.

For example: 'Any dispute must be brought to the attention of the supplier in writing within 14 days following receipt of goods'. Other terms may state that disputes are invalid if the payment due date on the original invoice has passed.

The problem is that few companies include these provisions. They are so grateful to receive an order, they start doing business without a contract, which sets them up to attract bad debt.

Smart operators include provisions in their terms and conditions that allude to: *'Directors of limited companies who fail to honour the sales terms and conditions can be held personally liable for any outstanding debts'*. This simple addition will help in the future because even if a debtor company fails to pay, you could effectively have a personal guarantee from the director(s).

For creditors, success in debt litigation depends mostly on how well their sales terms have been structured, specifically with regards to dealing with disputes. There is no way to prevent a customer from disputing an unpaid invoice. But including provisions to deal with disputes will help to protect your company from unscrupulous debtors, mainly because so few people read contracts before signing them.

For a creditor who has included the necessary provisions but still has trouble collecting payment of an overdue invoice, the next step is to seek a judgment from either a county or high court to confirm the debt and amount owed.

If the debtor fails to respond to further requests for payment, depending on the creditor's credit control procedures, they may send a letter before action, which is a formal document reminding the debtor their credit period has expired and requesting payment within seven days.

Statutory Demands and Winding-up Petitions

Similarly, the creditor may issue a statutory demand, which orders the debtor to pay within 21 days and is the first step in insolvency proceedings to wind up a limited company. After 21 days, the creditor is free to present to court a petition to have the debtor company wound up because they now have evidence of insolvency. But only if the debt is:

1. Undisputed
2. Worth £750 or more
3. Unpaid after 21 days

At this stage, the debtor has three options:

1. Arrange a schedule of payment with the creditor.
2. Pay the debt within 21 days.
3. Dispute the debt.

Disputed Debts

Disputes tend to arise when it is time to pay, usually after customers have received the goods or service. Even if there is no problem, some people will create one simply to pay a fraction of the debt or nothing at all. Consequently, debtors sometimes create disputes just to immobilise the creditor because a winding-up petition cannot be issued if the debt is disputed.

Avoid Shortcuts

When attempting to recover undisputed debts, if time permits, the first thing you should do is get a judgment debt order from either a county or high court. If the debtor ignores the judgment you have solid grounds to issue a winding-up petition. But few creditors take this route because it is lengthy and the debtor may disappear into a statutory insolvency process whereby you suffer significant loss.

Sometimes, issuing a winding-up petition without securing a court judgment can be a mistake because the debtor can claim to have no knowledge of the debt. In such circumstances, the judge may side with the debtor, and ask: 'Before coming here, why didn't you first go to the county court, try the facts and get your judgment?'

Counterclaims

Counterclaiming is another strategy sometimes utilised by debtors. For example, a villainous company director may say to a supplier to whom they owe £20,000:

'The service you delivered was so poor that I had to call another supplier who charged me £25,000 to do the job properly. As a result, I'm suing you for £25,000; so why don't we just call it quits and both walk away?'

To avoid becoming the victim of a debtor who counterclaims simply to avoid paying, include the following provision in your sales terms and conditions:

'Any claim made against our company may not be offset against any outstanding monies that are owed to the company.'

Debt Litigation

If you are confident the dispute has no merit, but the debtor still refuses to pay, the next step is litigation. If the debt is undisputed, a solicitor specialising in debt recovery may suffice.

Disputed debts require litigation lawyers, but they usually charge hourly rates over a fixed fee, which can be expensive. For example, a creditor chasing a £50,000 debt who applies to the county court for a judgment must first pay a court fee equal to 5% of the debt's value (£2,500). If the debtor responds by disputing the debt, a sensible creditor will hire a lawyer specialising in debt litigation who will probably charge somewhere in the region of £5,000.

If you are lucky and the action is launched in a rural area, the case should come up in around six months and you'll receive a favourable judgment at a cost of £7,500. However, in a more likely scenario, if you use a court in a city such as London, Birmingham, Bristol, Leeds or Cardiff, where staff are overworked and resources are stretched, the same case could take between nine and 18 months to be heard. Naturally, the lawyer will need compensation for the extra hours spent working on the case, which is likely to increase the creditor's expense bill to around £10,000.

If the debtor defends the claim and insists there is a genuine dispute, the courts will encourage the parties to enter mediation, which could take another three to four months. If that doesn't work, the case returns to court and the process continues.

Although some creditors are successful, issuing winding-up petitions without proper guidance and support can be a high-risk course of action because you may need to back off as soon as you're presented with a substantive dispute. Furthermore, the debtor can go bust at any time having benefited from your money interest-free.

ISSUING COUNTY COURT CLAIMS & CCJS

What is a County Court Money Claim?

Any person or business can apply to a county court to demand payment of an unpaid debt in accordance with Part 7 of the Ministry of Justice's Civil Procedure Rules. A claim takes place when an individual or business applies to a county court to demand payment of an unpaid debt from a company or person.

Before applying for a county court money claim a claimant should first serve the debtor with a pre-action letter. This is a formal notice explaining the circumstances surrounding the debt and requesting payment within 14 days. The claimant can make a county court money claim if the defendant fails to:

- Pay
- Reach an agreement to pay

The court fee, which must be paid in advance, depends on the amount of the claim. For example, the current cost is:

- £35 for a claim of £300 or less
- £205 if the claim is between £3,000 and £5,000
- £10,000 for claims that exceed £200,000

Fees are less expensive online but claims in excess of £100,000 can only be made via post. Proceedings commence when the court issues a claim form, which must be completed by the claimant along with the particulars of claim

(POC). The POC, which can be included on the claim form or attached separately, outlines exactly what the claim is about.

Upon receipt of payment, the claim form and POC, the court will process the action and issue a county court notice to be served on the defendant who has 14 days to acknowledge receipt. When a defendant fails to respond in time, they are deemed to have accepted the debt. This could lead the claimant to file a 'request for judgment' form for the court to order a judgment in default. Still, judgments in default can be set aside because the court has only heard from one party.

Mediation

When a claim has been defended, before scheduling hearing dates the court will write to both parties and suggest they try settling the dispute through mediation. They will recommend that both parties attend a mediation centre where they can share the costs for hiring a mediator at a rate of around £1,500 a day. Alternatively, each party is free to:

- Hire their own solicitors and barristers
- Go through the process unrepresented to keep costs down

If a settlement is reached, it is always good to draw up either a consent order or a Tomlin order to document details of the agreement, which becomes legally binding once the order has been received and sealed by the court. If mediation fails or breaks down, the parties return to court.

It is worth considering that if a claimant refuses to enter mediation, continues to prosecute the claim and wins, the defendant can argue they should not be held liable for the claimant's costs as both parties' expenses would have been reduced if they had entered mediation. In such circumstances, the court may:

- Agree and recommend the defendant pay none or a contribution to the costs

- Disagree and order the defendant to pay full costs

Directions Questionnaire

If you are bringing a claim and get past the mediation stage, before you go to trial the court will require both parties to fill out a directions questionnaire. This will help the court manage the case and decide whether the claim should be allocated to the small claims, fast track or multi track (see below).

The questionnaire is like a standard disclosure form that explains what the case is about and confirms details such as the:

- Documents each party will be disclosing
- Names of witnesses and experts who may be called to provide evidence

Small Claims

For small claims of less than £10,000, neither party is entitled to recover their costs. As a result, it is sometimes better for claimants to represent themselves as neither party will recoup their legal expenses.

For example, if a law firm charges £500 to issue a claim for a £9,000 debt, which is later defended, they may request further payment of £2,000 to £3,000 to litigate the claim through to trial. Even if the lawyers are successful, the claimant will still be out of pocket, having spent £2,000 to £3,000 recovering £9,000.

In contrast, defendants who represent themselves would be operating from a position of strength in negotiations because they have no litigation costs.

Fast Track and Multi Track

Fast-track claims are valued between £10,000 and £25,000. Although these claims are hurried through the system, they can take 12 to 18 months to go to trial depending on how busy the court is and the complexity of the case. Multi-track claims - for debts greater than £25,000 - are prioritised as they tend to be complex and involve more litigation.

Summary Judgment

A claimant who believes their opponent's defence is weak may apply to the court for a summary judgment, which asks the court to consider the claim based on the available evidence without going to trial.

Unless Order

Some defendants frustrate the process by deliberately failing to comply with court-issued directions. This forces the claimant to apply for an unless order, which declares that unless the defendant complies by a particular date their defence is liable to be struck out of court.

Unless orders sometimes backfire because even if a litigant wins or successfully defends a claim, the courts may order them to pay all the costs as they were the non-compliant party. Moreover, the defendant costs will increase every time they apply for a court order and the court may eventually order them to pay all costs on an interim basis. Under these circumstances, defendants can end up spending more in the long run if the court decides that all costs will be dealt with at the end of the trial.

Costs

County courts are loathed by claimants because even the most flimsy defence can buy a defendant an additional six months for a debt they had originally agreed to pay in 30 days. As a result, it is normal for claimants to spend £5,000 to

£10,000 trying to recover a £30,000 debt. Even if the claimant wins the case, by the end of the trial the debtor would have had their £30,000 for 12 to 18 months.

Moreover, it has become conventional that when the claimant tries to collect payment, they discover the debtor company has collapsed and reconstituted elsewhere. Consequently, claimants with undisputed debts often prefer to issue a winding-up petition as this action is swifter than the county court process.

Enforcing a Judgment

The most popular methods of enforcing a judgment are to either issue a winding-up petition or utilise the services of a bailiff (also known as Higher Court enforcement officer) who will:

- Attend the defendant's premises
- Take and sell whatever goods and stock they find
- Use the proceeds to pay the debt

Third-party Debt Order

A savvy claimant may apply for a third-party debt order, which allows them to collect money from a third party who owes the defendant.

For example, if a claimant who is owed £20,000 knows the defendant is about to collect £30,000 from a customer, they can use a third-party debt order to force the customer to pay the £20,000 debt. Furthermore, the customer will find themselves in contempt of court if they refuse.

A claimant who makes a third-party debt order for £20,000 against a bank must present the order on a day when the defendant's account has sufficient funds because the order will fail if the account is overdrawn. The order can only be used once, so if there is only £10,000 in the account the claimant must find another way to recover the remaining £10,000.

Charging Order

Alternatively, a claimant may apply for a charging order against a property owned by the defendant or their company. If the property is sold, the full amount of the charge (plus interest and any costs) must be paid before any proceeds are passed on to the creditor.

Additional Advice

Depending on the circumstance, it can be unwise to make a claim without first serving the defendant with a pre-action letter. This is because, irrespective of the outcome of the proceedings, it is unlikely the claimant will have their costs paid, as the defendant will say:

'These court proceedings are unnecessary because if the claimant had set out the claim in writing to me, I would have considered their request and paid the bill.'

A claimant who is chasing a sizeable debt but knows little about the defendant should consider applying to the court for an oral examination. This requires the defendant to attend a hearing to answer questions under oath about their income, assets, savings and expenditure. From the information disclosed, the claimant can decide which type of enforcement action will best help them recover the debt.

SERVING A STATUTORY DEMAND

How to Use a Statutory Demand

If a company or individual (the debtor) owes you (the creditor) an undisputed sum but has not paid or provided a reasonable explanation for the lack of payment, you should consider insolvency proceedings.

The first step in this process would be to serve them with a statutory demand. But you must act swiftly as your debtor may be:

- Paying other creditors instead of you
- Exposing you to suffer unnecessary loss
- Using your credit terms as an unsecured, interest-free loan
- Taking assets into a new company while leaving you and other creditors to perish with the old one
- Trading while insolvent
- On the brink of collapse

A statutory demand (stat demand or stat d) is a formal document requesting payment of an overdue debt within 21 days. You can serve a statutory demand on a company or person for any debt that is:

- Undisputed
- Fewer than six years old
- £750 or more (for a company)
- £5,000 or more (for an individual)

Formal Demands

Before commencing insolvency proceedings to wind up a limited company, you must first serve the debtor a statutory demand. Serving a winding-up petition after presenting a statutory demand will strengthen your case, but it isn't always necessary. Issuing of a formal demand is recommended, as it:

- Outlines the amount and circumstances of the debt
- Threatens the serving of a winding-up petition unless payment is made within 14, seven or five days

Why Should They Pay?

Failure to respond to either a formal demand or a statutory demand could result in the winding up of a limited company or bankruptcy for an individual.

Winding-up Petition

You are free to serve a winding-up petition on a limited company 21 days after presenting your statutory demand. But only if:

- The debt remains unpaid
- No arrangement has been made to pay
- The statutory demand has neither been withdrawn nor set aside

A debtor company that ignores a winding-up petition may have its bank account(s) frozen.

HOW TO MAKE A PERSON BANKRUPT

Traditionally, there has been a stigma attached to bankruptcy. Consequently, forcing a debtor into bankruptcy may be a viable option if you are having trouble collecting an outstanding debt. A creditor's bankruptcy petition is an application to the court to seize and sell the assets of a person with debts of £5,000 or more.

Before presenting a debtor with a bankruptcy petition, you (the creditor) must first serve a statutory demand. If the debtor neither pays nor reaches an agreement to pay, you can present a bankruptcy petition; currently costing £1,270 including the court fee. The petition should be filed in the county court nearest to where the debtor resides. A court may make a bankruptcy order if they decide the debtor is insolvent. The procedure is almost identical to a debtor's bankruptcy petition. The debtor is summoned by the official receiver for an examination and an insolvency practitioner (trustee) may be appointed.

Bankruptcy can affect a person's credit rating for up to six years and they will be unable to obtain credit of more than £250 without disclosing their bankruptcy. Bankrupts still have to pay court fines, student loans and child maintenance, and the trustee may sell some of their most valuable assets to pay creditors. Furthermore, after the respondent (debtor) has been bankrupt for one year, the trustee can try to seize and sell their home if there is significant equity in the property.

Trustees

The function of a trustee (insolvency practitioner) in bankruptcy is comparable to that of an administrator or liquidator in the insolvency of a limited company. Irrespective of the procedure, the insolvency practitioner's main task is to realise assets to pay creditors. Aside from the tools of the debtor's trade, absolutely everything else is up for grabs. Creditors are free to remove and replace the trustee with a licensed insolvency practitioner of their choice.

IPOs and IPAs

If a trustee believes the debtor has surplus income, they can ask the court to make the debtor pay up to 36 monthly payments into the bankruptcy estate via an income payments order (IPO). Alternatively, you can make these payments voluntarily through an income payment agreement (IPA). The fee for both is approximately £150, which will be taken out of your first payment.

BRUs and BROs

Bankrupts who accept accusations of misconduct usually agree to sign a bankruptcy restriction undertaking (BRU), which extends the bankruptcy conditions for an additional three or four years. But if a bankrupt challenges allegations of misconduct, their trustee and creditors may apply for a bankruptcy restriction order (BRO), which can extend the bankruptcy for up to 15 years.

WINDING-UP PETITIONS

A winding-up petition is the commencement of formal insolvency proceedings whereby the petition creditor obtains a court order that forces an insolvent company into compulsory liquidation.

Talk to the Debtor

The period before, during and after the commencement of a formal insolvency procedure can be very stressful. You should talk to the debtor as they may be open to negotiating a deal to avoid their company being wound up. Strictly speaking, under these circumstances, all payments and any use of the company's assets should be validated by the court once a winding-up petition has been issued.

Consequences of a Winding-up Petition

The serving of a winding-up petition should concern a company director because section 127 of the Insolvency Act 1986 is immediately triggered. Under section 127, directors are forbidden from taking several actions, including making payments from the company's bank account(s) without first obtaining the court's permission.

Failure to respond to the winding-up petition or obtain a validation order may result in:

- The freezing of the company's bank account(s)
- The petition being advertised in *The London Gazette* newspaper

Furthermore, if the company is wound up, the director will become personally liable for all transactions and payments made from the bank account(s) after the issuing of the winding-up petition. To avoid the company being wound up, they can pay the debt before the court hearing as this demonstrates the business is solvent and able to pay its debts when they are due.

Although you should never abuse a winding-up petition as an instrument of debt recovery, it is perfectly okay to issue them against insolvent companies who fail to pay debts when due.

Disputed Debts

If the debtor responds by applying for and obtaining a validation order from the court, your winding-up petition will probably be dismissed when the case is heard and you may be ordered to pay all the costs. At this stage, a sensible petitioner will agree to the winding-up petition being dismissed and tell the debtor:

'I'll withdraw the petition. But you need to pay my costs because you failed to mention the dispute when I initially requested payment and sent a formal demand.'

It is an abuse of court to issue a winding-up petition for a disputed debt, so you must immediately withdraw your petition if the debtor provides evidence of a genuine dispute. But sometimes debtors are so daunted by the prospect of litigation and the potential closure of their business, they simply pay up.

Certificate of Compliance

There are usually four weeks between the issuing of a winding-up petition and the first hearing. At least five working days before the hearing, you must complete and file with the court a certificate of compliance, which verifies that all the court's rules and procedures have been complied with. The certificate should include information confirming:

- The petition was served and advertised correctly
- A list of creditors who support and oppose the petition

Alternative Dispute Resolutions

You should always ensure that alternative dispute resolutions are included in sales documents when establishing a relationship with a new debtor. A savvy creditor will have the following provisions written somewhere on their invoices, orders, delivery notes and terms of supply:

'Any dispute must be brought to the attention of the supplier in writing within 14 days following receipt of goods.

'All goods on the supplier's terms only, and by taking delivery of supplied goods you accept the supplier's terms and conditions as binding and final.'

These provisions are essential as they prevent debtors from creating bogus disputes and help to ensure swift payment of goods and services offered on credit.

COMPANY VOLUNTARY ARRANGEMENT (CVA)

What is a CVA?

A company voluntary arrangement (CVA) is a formal contract between an insolvent company and its creditors. It allows a company to continue trading while repaying its creditors, usually over a period of three to five years.

Benefits of a CVA

Creditors often ask if it would be better to place the company into liquidation and sell the assets to repay them. But creditors are never better off in liquidation; creditors in company voluntary arrangements (CVAs) always receive more. Furthermore, in liquidation there is no possibility of generating income from future business.

However, if the company is doing well and profits are soaring three years into a CVA, the insolvency practitioner who facilitates the arrangement can increase the amount creditors receive in their periodic payments.

Entering a CVA

The process begins when a company's director seeks out and hires an insolvency practitioner, known as a nominee, to put together a company voluntary arrangement proposal. Depending on the size of the company, most small and medium-sized enterprises (SMEs) can expect a nominee to charge between £8,000 and £15,000 to prepare a proposal, which takes two to four weeks to prepare and usually includes:

- Financial data
- A synopsis of the company's trading history
- Information about the directors, creditors, shareholders and employees
- Three- to five-year restructuring projections explaining how the business will become profitable and pay monthly into the CVA

Additionally, the proposal sets out the fees charged by the nominee who becomes a 'supervisor' after the terms have been ratified. Supervisors usually charge small and medium-sized enterprises £30,000 to £40,000 to collect periodical monthly sums, which they distribute to creditors once or twice a year.

The director(s) sign off the proposal in the form of a sworn affidavit, and a creditors' meeting is convened. In the affidavit, the nominee will state to creditors: *'...the proposal is fit, fair and feasible, and has a good chance of success.'*

If the company falls into more than two months' arrears on their contributions to creditors, the CVA will be deemed to have failed and the supervisor will be obliged to apply to the court to wind up the company by a compulsory court order.

Ironically, insolvency practitioners rarely tell creditors the proposal will fail even though around 50% of companies that enter CVAs fall into liquidation within five years, which suggests that a worrying number of insolvency practitioners are overly optimistic.

How is a CVA Proposal Approved?

A group of creditors who are owed at least 75% of the debt must vote in favour of the proposal for a CVA to be approved. They can do this via email, virtual meetings or some other correspondence.

Connected Creditors

After friends and relatives of the director(s) who have lent money to the company (connected creditors) are removed from the equation, 50% of the remaining creditors must be in favour for the proposal to be successful.

How to Block a CVA

A coalition comprising 26% of the creditors is required to either block the CVA or push through modifications to the proposal.

Top Tips

Creditors should never automatically accept the director(s)' choice of nominee or their CVA proposal because it is almost impossible for an insolvency practitioner to prioritise creditors' interests over those of the director(s) who appointed them. Frequently, a director seeking a CVA will approach an insolvency practitioner and say something like:

'I've got £1m worth of debt, but only want to pay out £500,000', and together they will fashion a set of financial figures to demonstrate there is only enough revenue to pay creditors £500,000. In reality, there may be another £500,000 hidden in the figures, stock or elsewhere in the company's assets.

Of course, if the insolvency practitioner refuses to facilitate the director(s)' requirements, they will simply find a more accommodating nominee elsewhere.

Subsequently, it is essential that creditors insist on modifications to the CVA proposal. The first change they make should be to appoint their own insolvency practitioner/supervisor.

Removing the Nominee

Too few creditors are aware of their rights or realise how much power they hold. Creditors can remove the nominee and appoint their own insolvency practitioner before the proposal is approved if they are:

- Dissatisfied with the supervisor
- Uncomfortable with the supervisor's relationship with the company director(s) In most instances, creditors' interests are best served after they have replaced the insolvency practitioner chosen by the company director(s) with one they have appointed. Creditors' leverage is even greater if they unite and communicate in the weeks, days and hours before the proposal is ratified.

Creditors who ask for the insolvency practitioner to be removed can expect the director(s) to insist on keeping the supervisor in exchange for increasing the amount of money the company puts into the CVA. This response would suggest a director has something to hide and would therefore be open to some form of compromise and negotiation.

On the other hand, the director(s) may respond by allowing the company to collapse into liquidation. Although no one wants this to happen, creditors must nevertheless press for modifications to the proposal that will ultimately increase the amount they receive.

For example, if the proposal recommends paying creditors 35p in every £1, it is perfectly okay for them to ask for modifications that request:

- 50p in every £1
- A reduction in the supervisor's fees

- Payouts every three months rather than twice a year

Creditors effectively pay the fees of the insolvency practitioner because the money used to pay nominees and supervisors would otherwise be redistributed to them. Most creditors overlook how an insolvency practitioner's fees can spiral over time.

For example, if a company agrees to pay £5,000 a month into the CVA and the supervisor charges a monthly fee of £500 over five years, they would take home £30,000, which is:

- A lot of money
- A little excessive
- Something very few creditors would pick up on

CREDITORS' VOLUNTARY LIQUIDATION (CVL)

Although the process is called a creditors' voluntary liquidation (CVL), it is the director who decides whether or not the company is able to meet its obligations and commitments.

Meeting of Shareholders

If the director decides the company is insolvent, they must:

- Call a meeting of shareholders
- Convince 75% of shareholders to wind up the company
- Nominate an insolvency practitioner to coordinate the liquidation

Insolvency practitioners act as liquidators on behalf of the court and have far-reaching statutory duties.

Deemed Consent

The first responsibility of the nominated insolvency practitioner is to contact all the creditors. They will be informed that on a given date (usually within seven to 10 days), the company will be deemed to have gone into liquidation. Unless creditors call for a physical meeting of creditors, they are deemed to have accepted the decision to make the company insolvent.

Role of the Liquidator

The four main functions of a liquidator are to:

- Secure all assets
- Realise those assets as cash
- Transfer cash into the liquidation estate
- Distribute funds from the estate equally among creditors

Statement of Affairs

Following their investigations, the liquidator will produce a Statement of Insolvency Practice 6 report, which offers brief insight into how the company started, what it does and how it became insolvent.

The report, which is made available to creditors prior to the liquidation date, must include a statement of affairs comprising:

- Statutory data
- Information about any legal proceedings
- Consolidated accounts for the previous three years
- A summarised version of management accounts from the last accounting period up to the present date
- The company's trading history
- Reasons for the company's failure

Additionally, the report, which is to be confirmed and signed-off by the director(s), includes:

- A schedule describing the company's assets
- An estimate of the realised value of those assets
- A list detailing the name and address of each creditor and how much they are owed.

Once the liquidation expenses have been met, the surplus is distributed to creditors in order of priority. Secured creditors are paid first, then preferential creditors receive payment, then any remaining money is distributed equally among unsecured creditors. When the liquidator has completed the insolvency process the company is dissolved.

How Are Creditors Affected?

When a business falls into insolvency, two of the most important concerns for creditors should be:

1) Who is the liquidator?
2) How much are their fees?

Although the director(s) choose the liquidator, it is the creditors who appoint them and effectively pay for the liquidation. As a result, it is important to find out as much as you can about the liquidator as soon as possible. Try to ensure they have no prior relationship with the director(s).

Creditors' Meetings

Shortly before or after the commencement of a statutory insolvency procedure, the insolvency practitioner will convene a meeting of creditors (also known as a creditors' meeting). Unless creditors ask for a physical meeting, they are deemed to have accepted the decision to make the company insolvent.

However, the director(s) must consent if a physical meeting is requested by:

- 10 creditors
- 10% of creditors
- 10% of creditors by value

At the creditors' meeting, creditors have an opportunity to:

- Appoint their own insolvency practitioner/liquidator
- Set the liquidator's remuneration
- Ask questions
- Compel the liquidator to take action
- Form a creditors' committee to oversee and assist the liquidator

Creditors' Committees

Unsecured creditors can gain greater control over the liquidation by uniting and forming a creditors' committee because there is strength in numbers. The committee:

- Comprises three to five elected creditors
- Assists the liquidator
- Approves the liquidator's remuneration and generally increases transparency Normally, liquidators perform their duties with little supervision, updating creditors on progress every six to 12 months. However, when a committee is in place, creditors can insist that a liquidator attend meetings every three or six months to provide feedback.

Replacing the Insolvency Practitioner

In many cases, the liquidation process could be more favourable to creditors. But for this to happen they must become more proactive and aware of their powers. In a creditors' voluntary liquidation, replacing the insolvency practitioner is usually the best course of action because the liquidator should be working in the interest of creditors, rather than on behalf of the director(s) who gave them the job.

Creditors are far more likely to enhance their prospects for dividends when they appoint their own insolvency practitioner. However, if they fail to use the power of their votes at creditors' meetings, the director(s)' choice of liquidator is invariably appointed. Moreover, creditors may need a liquidator who will investigate the director(s) thoroughly and robustly, but this can be challenging if they are associated in any way.

Similarly, it is always best to scrutinise and question the liquidator's costs because the more they charge the less likely it is that creditors will receive any monies back. In far too many instances, unsecured creditors receive little or no money because the funds in the liquidation estate have been eaten up by the liquidator's fees.

Most creditors are completely blind to the shenanigans of self-serving insolvency practitioners, and those who are aware have become apathetic after going through previous liquidations and never get anything back. Nevertheless, in essence, creditors are partly responsible for the liquidator's pay and this is where much of their power lies.

Creditors who decide to hire their own liquidator must act swiftly because once the date of the first creditors' meeting is announced they will have only a few days to unite and form a group to overturn the director(s)' nomination.

A coalition of creditors comprising at least 50% of voters is required to reject the liquidator, and appoint a replacement. When creditors fail to use the power of their votes at creditors' meetings, invariably the director(s)' choice of liquidator is appointed.

Fixing a Liquidator's Fees

Liquidators tend to charge on a time cost basis, but it is perfectly okay for creditors to suggest alternatives. For example, they could propose a remuneration package comprising a mixture of an hourly fee and a percentage of the revenue from the sale of the company's assets and realisations from investigations. Equally, creditors may request that a percentage of the realised funds be ring-fenced for unsecured creditors.

COMPULSORY LIQUIDATION

What is Compulsory Liquidation?

The process of a compulsory liquidation usually starts when an unpaid creditor files a winding-up petition in court against a company they believe is insolvent. If a judge agrees to make the order, the case is sent to the official receiver, a court official employed by the government's Insolvency Service.

After the official receiver confirms there are assets to realise and investigations to conduct, they will nominate an insolvency practitioner to liquidate the company. The liquidator will:

- Terminate contracts (automatic procedure for all contracts)
- Realise the company's assets
- Conduct investigations into the company's affairs
- Report to the Insolvency Service on the director(s)' conduct

The first responsibility of the official receiver is to contact all the creditors of the company. They will be informed that on a given date the company was, by compulsory order, wound-up by the court and entered into liquidation. Unless creditors call for a physical meeting of creditors, they are deemed to have accepted the official receiver's decision to keep the job, or nominate an insolvency practitioner (IP).

Liquidators analyse transactions to establish if they were made in the interest of the creditors. Four of a liquidator's main functions are to:

1) Secure all assets
2) Realise those assets as cash
3) Transfer the cash into the liquidation estate
4) Distribute funds from the estate equally to creditors

Appointment of the Liquidator

If creditors meet the requirements, the official receiver will call a creditors' meeting to appoint a liquidator. But creditors must act swiftly. After the date of the first creditors' meeting has been announced, they only have a few days to form a group to replace the nominated liquidator with their own insolvency practitioner.

Creditors'/Liquidation Committee

Unsecured creditors can gain greater control over the liquidation by uniting and forming a creditors' committee because there is strength in numbers.

The committee, which comprises between three and five elected creditors:

- Assists the liquidator
- Approves their remuneration
- Generally increases transparency

Normally, liquidators perform their duties with little supervision, updating creditors on progress every 12 months. However, when a committee is in place, creditors can insist that a liquidator attend meetings every six months to provide feedback.

Appointing Your Own Liquidator

A coalition of creditors comprising at least 50% of voters is required to reject the liquidator, and appoint a replacement. Creditors are far more likely to enhance their prospects for dividends when they appoint their own liquidator. However, the opportunity is missed if they fail to use the power of their votes at creditors' meetings.

Conclusion

In many ways, the new insolvency rules that came into effect in April 2017 enable the liquidation process to run more efficiently. However, there are many unsympathetic liquidators who take the view that suppliers with unsecured debts are foolish for giving credit and failing to do due diligence on a struggling company. Creditors should engage in the insolvency process as soon as they are notified of a procedure to maximise leverage, and improve dividend prospects.

CREDITORS' GUIDE TO ADMINISTRATION

What is Administration?

Administration is a procedure that functions as a rescue mechanism for asset-rich but insolvent companies and is usually a precursor or alternative to liquidation. The procedure allows a business to be:

- Rescued as a going concern
- Sold as whole
- Offloaded in parts to realise cash for creditors

Difference Between Administration and Liquidation

Liquidation is the end of the road, similar to switching off a company's life support machine. In contrast, entering administration is like being connected to a life support machine, the company may:

- Expire
- Be sold as a going concern
- Continue to exist through either a pre-pack administration or a company voluntary arrangement (CVA)

Generally, administrations are expensive and quickly devour a company's cash leaving very little, if anything, for creditors. Administration normally results in a company's swift demise, especially if the business cannot be sold immediately as a going concern.

Administration Order

Following an application to court for an administration order, there are three ways a company can be placed into administration:

- In court
- Out of court
- If a charge holder (creditor) invites an administrator (insolvency practitioner) to act as interim chief executive with custodial responsibility for the company's obligations and assets

Charge Holder

A charge is a secured loan, similar to a mortgage, which companies may grant to any third party. Charge holders are usually banks or some other financial institution. A company may grant a charge over its assets in exchange for cash and/or credit. Thereafter, the company enters a covenant with the charge holder, agreeing to repay the loan by meeting a series of contractual obligations.

Floating Charge Debenture

If the covenant (usually a floating charge debenture) is breached, the charge holder may appoint an administrator to take control of the relevant assets - without notifying the company's director(s).

For example, a charge holder who discovers the company has been served with a winding-up petition can protect themselves by appointing an administrator to:

- Take control of the assets under the charge
- Realise those assets for the benefit of the charge holder

Administration Procedures

The director(s) of a company they deem insolvent may also activate an out-of-court administration. This involves:

- Filing an application to the court
- Making and signing an affidavit or witness statement
- Calling in an insolvency practitioner to confirm the company's insolvency

Court Administration

Directors or creditors can present evidence of the company's insolvency to activate a court administration. Creditors and other third parties can object when the application is heard by a court judge.

Creditors are free to contact the administrator and arrange to purchase the business in part or as a whole. They must put in tenders and the administrator is likely to sell the business to the highest bidder. Alternatively, a director can cleanse the business by arranging to purchase some or all of its assets in a pre-pack administration.

Pre-Pack Administration

Since the introduction of the Enterprise Act by Tony Blair's government in 2002, unscrupulous directors have used the legislation to:

- Run up masses of debt
- Place their business into administration
- Use a pre-pack administration to buy the assets back from the administrator without any of the debts, liabilities or creditors

There are at least two conflict-of-interest issues for the administrator and company director(s) in a pre-pack:

1) The administrator's employment depends largely on whether their valuation of the business is agreeable to the director(s)

2) The director(s) act as both seller and buyer

Subsequently, if the director(s) are unhappy with the appraisal, they are unlikely to hire the administrator to coordinate the pre-pack.

Tips for Creditors

Pre-pack administrations are tricky. This is because the first time unsecured creditors usually become aware of the procedure is when the administrator notifies them around seven days later. A side from duediligence and being cautious of who you give credit to, the best thing creditors can do to protect themselves is galvanize.

Perhaps even more frustrating is that if permitted to pay in instalments, directors essentially use the cash due to creditors to buy the business back; the income generated from this new venture will be used to pay for the administration costs, which consists mostly of the insolvency practitioner's expenses.

Above all, as soon as you hear about the administration you should encourage other creditors and suppliers to quickly arrange a creditors' meeting. Additionally, you will find that forming a committee of creditors offers several advantages.

Creditors must try to replace the administrator. This is because in a pre-pack, no matter what the insolvency practitioner says, it is almost impossible for them to prioritise creditors' interests over those of the director(s). Creditors should appoint their own insolvency practitioner. But there must be enough assets in the business to pay an incoming administrator.

The liquidator should review the administrator's work, and try to establish whether the business was sold for too little. If that can be proved, the new insolvency practitioner can sue the first administrator, but that is difficult because the business would have been valued by professional appraisers.

Subsequently, the incoming insolvency practitioner must review the files and look for things such as preferential payments, transactions at undervalue and any other misfeasance. An insolvency practitioner who discovers such transgressions will chase the director(s) for antecedent transactions and try to bring more revenue into the estate for creditors.

CREDITORS' MEETINGS

A creditors' meeting (also known as a meeting of creditors) is usually convened shortly after a company becomes insolvent to:

- Explain what went wrong
- Appoint an insolvency practitioner (IP)
- Agree the insolvency practitioner's fees
- Vote on how to move forward with the business

Creditors' voluntary liquidations (CVLs) commence with a virtual or physical meeting of creditors. This meeting must convene no more than seven days after creditors receive notification of the liquidation.

The procedure is slightly different for creditors in administration, if a company enters a company voluntary arrangement (CVA) or when a person utilises an individual voluntary arrangement (IVA). In these instances, the meeting of creditors takes place within 14 days of the proposal being distributed. Similarly, the creditors' meeting takes place within 10 weeks of the date the company entered into administration.

According to a report on corporate insolvency published by the Office of Fair Trading in 2010, very few unsecured creditors had any real understanding of the purpose of a creditors' meeting or how an insolvency practitioner is appointed. Invariably, creditors tend to be apathetic because so few have ever received anything like a sensible dividend from previous insolvencies.

There are no legal guidelines or restrictions with regards to remuneration for insolvency practitioners. As a result, they will discourage you from attending by charging an excessive amount to hold creditors' meetings. However, the first physical meeting of creditors is where creditors can get empowered and develop an insolvency strategy.

Few creditors really understand how much power they wield because the insolvency practitioner who coordinates the procedure is their employee. The insolvency practitioner only does the job to get paid and it is the creditors who determine the terms, conditions and rate of pay. So, who is in control of the situation?

Fixing an Insolvency Practitioner's Fees

If there is no committee of creditors to set fees, creditors automatically accept the insolvency practitioner's remuneration package by deemed consent. For example, once a creditors' committee has been established, if an insolvency practitioner intends to charge £400 per hour, creditors can say:

'No way, we've found someone who'll do the job for £200 an hour. Reduce your fees by at least 50% or we're going to appoint them, which will require the requisition and convening of another creditors' meeting solely for the purpose of insolvency practitioner's removal.'

Replacing an Insolvency Practitioner

Ideally, the choice of insolvency practitioner should rest with creditors. However, in most cases the insolvent appoints the insolvency practitioner simply because creditors fail to use the power of their votes at creditors' meetings.

If creditors are dissatisfied with the insolvency practitioner and 50% of voters in value and in attendance (including by proxy) agree, creditors can replace the insolvency practitioner with one of their own choice.

Generally, creditor-appointed insolvency practitioners tend to:

- Charge lower fees
- Offer higher rates of return for unsecured creditors
- Investigate directors without fear or favour

However, creditors must act swiftly if they want to remove the insolvency practitioner because they will start racking up fees and consuming as much cash as possible if there is any hint or suspicion of another insolvency practitioner's involvement.

Committee of Creditors

The committee of creditors' main objective should be to separate the director(s) from the insolvency practitioner to ensure they are working in the creditors' interest.

Although insolvency practitioners have a statutory obligation to inform creditors about the purpose and functions of a creditors' committee, very few encourage the formation of these groups because they really do not want anyone controlling their earnings or gaining too much insight into what they are doing. As a result, you will most likely find information about creditors' committees somewhere on one of the documents and leaflets supplied by the insolvency practitioner, possibly in small print on the very last page.

MAKING A MISFEASANCE CLAIM

What is Misfeasance?

Misfeasance takes place when a director or ex-director has misapplied, misappropriated, retained or become accountable for any of the company's money or property. Although the director and company are recognised as separate legal entities, in many instances the director is also a company employee.

Just like any other employee, directors must be seen to be putting the company's interest ahead of their own. Moreover, a director must always act with honesty and integrity and in a way that swells the company's assets. Misfeasance is far worse than maladministration because it means a director has been dishonest and engaged in bad behaviour, wrongdoing or some misconduct that's brought financial loss to creditors.

Who Can Bring a Misfeasance Claim?

Creditors, shareholders, and the liquidator may take misfeasance action against the director of a liquidated company. But no claim can be made if the business has entered administration or a company voluntary arrangement (CVA).

In the vast majority of cases, the insolvency practitioner (liquidator) brings a misfeasance action against the director. This usually happens because the liquidator has seen an opportunity to secure a recovery for creditors, and enrich themselves and the lawyers they work with. Subsequently, the court may limit the amount insolvency practitioners and lawyers can receive from a particular case to ensure creditors benefit from the proceeds.

Examples of Misfeasance

A director who removes assets from a company, or sells them to a friend at an undervalue price commits a misfeasance. other examples include:

- Making a preferential payments to creditors
- Failing to repay a director's loan
- Avoidance of property dispositions
- Misconduct during the course of winding-up proceedings

Sometimes a director's transgression may cause the company to be wound up, while in other cases the director only starts misbehaving after realising the company is insolvent.

Class Actions

A creditor who is considering legal action against a director should remember that misfeasance is a class remedy, so the claim will be brought on behalf of all creditors. As a result, any monies the court orders the director to pay must be shared equally among all the company's creditors.

For example, a creditor who is owed £50,000 may launch proceedings against the director of an insolvent company that owes 20 creditors £20,000 each, a total of £400,000. If the claim is successful and a court orders the director to make restitution of £100,000 into the company's liquidation estate, the creditor will get back only £5,000 as any disbursement must be shared equally with the other 19 creditors.

Additionally, the liquidation costs (which may include fees for lawyers and litigation funders) must be paid first. As a result, the net return for the creditor will probably be less significant.

Creditor Action

A creditor who brings a successful misfeasance action without the aid of an insolvency practitioner/liquidator can ask the court to ring-fence a specific amount for unsecured creditors. But if the action is successful and the liquidation is ongoing, an unscrupulous liquidator can easily take over the proceedings and gobble up the income.

Consequently, before launching an action it is sometimes better to wait until the liquidator has filed their Directors' Conduct D-Report, which is a confidential document about the director's behaviour that is delivered online to the Insolvency Service.

If a liquidator claimed to have no knowledge of misfeasance but creditors later found this to be untrue, it would be fair to describe the insolvency practitioner as 'incompetent' or 'deceitful'. Similarly, if a D-Report has been filed without any disclosures of wrongdoing it would be difficult for a liquidator to take over a misfeasance action because any misconduct should have been noted in their report.

Alternatively, a creditor looking to get back all, rather than a percentage, of their money should wait until the company has been dissolved and the liquidator released from office before advancing their misfeasance action.

Liquidator Action

If an insolvency practitioner or liquidator looks hard enough, they are likely to find misconduct in a lot of insolvency cases because an entrepreneurial director will always continue to do business in the belief they can trade themselves out of trouble. As a result, it is usually quite easy to identify dates and periods prior to the insolvency when a director could have and should have stopped trading to limit any losses to creditors.

Such evidence of insolvency can be established if the company had, for example:

- Unsatisfied county court judgments
- Made payments every 60 days to creditors who invoiced every 30 days

A competent insolvency practitioner will chronicle the company's bank statements and try to identify a pattern of preferential payments to connected suppliers and lenders who the director is friendly with.

If a liquidator has evidence that a company director continued to trade despite long periods of insolvency, which caused creditors to suffer loss, they may approach the director and try to make them pay money into the liquidation estate.

Deals Between the Director and Liquidator

If a company director owes £200,000 but decides to acknowledge only £50,000 of debt, the insolvency practitioner/liquidator can:

- Accept the payment
- Negotiate for more money
- Go to court

An insolvency practitioner who decides to litigate will have access to plenty of law firms, but limited resources to fund the action. Nevertheless, they work closely with lawyers so it is easy for them to get one to send the director a letter before action.

Additionally, the liquidator may seek the assistance of a litigation funder who will fund the case in exchange for around 30% to 50% of the proceeds. But this only happens if there is clear evidence of misfeasance and the director has a lot of cash. Liquidators are fearful of launching court proceedings without a litigation funder, losing and then having to explain why creditors' money was used to fund an unsuccessful action.

In the vast majority of cases, unless creditors and shareholders pursue the director(s) independently the outcome is more or less the same. The liquidator and their associates consume most of the proceeds and unsecured creditors are left with little or nothing at all. When a liquidator sends a letter before action and starts probing for money, some directors capitulate quickly and cut a deal, while others need more convincing.

How to Use Misfeasance to Your Advantage

In some cases, the court will order a director to pay creditors after the liquidator has been released from office. When this happens, the court may recall the liquidator to distribute the funds.

Rather than waiting for the action to advance and the court to find judgment, a clever creditor who is looking to get all their money back will approach the director and try to strike an independent deal.

Letter Before Action

The first step to launching a misfeasance claim is to engage in pre-action protocol by composing and sending to the director a letter before action, which:

- Describes the complaint
- Outlines the amount owed to the creditor

- Details the total sum owed to all creditors
- Must be responded to within 14 days

Make a Misfeasance Action

The misfeasance proceedings procedure involves filing an application to the court and providing a witness statement with supporting documents and exhibits. But first, the creditor must obtain leave from the court to file the application. After it is approved, the court will issue the application and provide as many sealed copies as necessary to be served on the company's director(s).

No matter how tough and unwavering a director is, they usually start taking the creditor seriously after receiving notification of misfeasance proceedings and observing the:

- Application form
- Witness statements
- Exhibits
- Court seal
- Case reference number
- Court hearing date

For example, when a creditor who lost £50,000 launches a misfeasance claim against a director whose company owes 20 creditors a total of £400,000, the director has three options:

1) Settle with all 20 creditors by paying £400,000 into the liquidation estate.

2) Prepare for a lengthy trial that could cost more than £100,000.

3) Pay the creditor's £50,000 debt and ask them to withdraw the action.

Now is the perfect time for the creditor who has launched the action to approach the director and negotiate a third-party payment. In these circumstances, the creditor has greater leverage if the evidence of misfeasance is compelling and the director has funds.

Any disbursement that comes directly from the proceeds of the insolvent company is a preferential payment. However, it is perfectly legal for a person unconnected to the action and company to make a one-off disbursement (paid either as a single sum or in installments), as this would simply be a third-party payment to reimburse the creditor in recognition of their loss. Once the director agrees, the creditor should get them to sign a non-disclosure agreement so the details of the deal remain confidential.

In these circumstances, the creditor must act quickly and discreetly because the liquidation is still ongoing, so the liquidator can either take over or join the action at the earliest opportunity, usually at the first court hearing.

Consequently, a creditor that successfully negotiates a payment should immediately go to court to avoid any obstructions from the liquidator. At court, they should apply to withdraw the misfeasance action or apply for a consent order to confirm they have agreed to discontinue the proceedings.

BRINGING A PROFESSIONAL NEGLIGENCE CLAIM

Professional negligence claims usually come about when a professional fails to deliver the duty of care they are supposed to provide. Although the list of vocations is extensive, lawyers, accountants, architects and doctors are particularly susceptible to professional negligence claims because in order to practise they must have professional indemnity insurance.

Making a Claim

When a professional negligence claim is made against a professional with indemnity insurance, their lawyers will step in and take over the case. Insurance lawyers have deep pockets and will drag out court proceedings trying to outspend and ultimately defeat the claimant. Nevertheless, your professional negligence claim is likely to be successful if you can clearly prove that:

- A professional owed you a duty of care
- That duty of care was breached
- The breach caused you sustained loss

In most cases, it helps if your claim is a class action because one person's allegation is subjective, but the same accusation will be taken more seriously if 20 others say they have experienced the same problem.

The type of debt claim being made will determine which protocols a claimant should adhere to in accordance with the practice directions of the Civil Procedure Rules 1998.

Pre-Action Letters

Usually for professional negligence claims, the claimant should write and send a detailed and fully compliant pre-action letter to the professional that includes:

- The claim's legal basis
- The facts and allegation
- Any supporting documents

The professional must acknowledge receipt within 28 days. The claimant can issue court proceedings or consider mediation if they are unhappy with the professional's response.

Mediation

After legal proceedings commence, the court will promote the idea of mediation to free up time for other cases and limit costs. A large number of claims are settled in mediation because it's something people only enter in to when they are in the frame of mind to agree, compromise and find the middle ground.

Going to Trial

The success of a professional negligence claim generally comes down to evidence and causation, that is, what grounds does the claimant have to bring a breach of duty claim? The case is definitely worth pursuing if the claimant can demonstrate a clear breach of duty, which has caused them to suffer some sustained loss. Additionally, the more evidence a claimant can gather to confirm both the breach of duty and the loss, the stronger their case will be.

Court proceedings normally commence with the disclosure and exchange of evidence. This is usually followed by a case management conference to provide direction for both parties and a timetable scheduling the dates for things they must do, such as: File evidence, Make applications, Submit budget costings to the court.

Funding

A claimant who is up against a formidable opponent will probably need someone to fund their claim. For example, even if a claimant has a really strong claim worth £1 million, the insurance company will never say: *'Yes, they're right; we're going to give them the money they're asking for.'*

Instead, they are far more likely to pay a law firm £250,000 and instruct them to *'get rid of the claim'*. And those lawyers will develop a strategy to defeat the action, simply by outspending the claimant.

Although the claimant may have a £1 million claim, if at any stage the defendant's lawyers make contact and say: *'Here's £250,000, take the money and walk away'*, the claimant may want to accept their offer or negotiate upwards because who knows what will happen at the end of the court claim. They may get lucky and win or it could take another year to discover they have lost the claim.

LITIGATION FUNDING

What is Litigation Funding?

Litigation funding takes place when a third party finances a court claim for commercial gain. This service empowers and enables claimants who would otherwise be disenfranchised to get justice, especially in professional negligence claims.

Generally, there are three common ways a claimant with no money but a strong case can pursue a claim and secure the services of a lawyer:

1) A conditional fee agreement (CFA)
2) A damage-based agreement (DBA)
3) Litigation funding

Whereas lawyers in a damage-based agreement take a percentage of whatever the court awards or is agreed in mediation, legal representatives in a CFA work on a no win, no fee basis, so their earnings vary depending on the outcome of the case. CFA lawyers are pretty easy to come by, although the claimant will still have to pay for counsel advice, which usually costs between £2,500 and £10,000, depending on the claim and its complexity.

However, for a claimant with a winnable case, another option is to hire a litigation funder. They will provide the claimant with litigation funds in the form of a loan, with interest charged at commercial rates or via an income- based model.

Litigation should really be the last option because no one can foretell the outcome of a trial, so they are always risky. In most instances, a litigant with a successful claim can expect to receive at least 50% of whatever the court awards and the remainder will pay for the lawyers and litigation funder.

How Does Litigation Funding Work?

Essentially, litigation funders want to know they have a good chance of succeeding. Subsequently, before considering whether to fund a case they will seek and retain the services of an experienced lawyer. The claimant and/or their solicitor will pass the evidence they have gathered on to a barrister, advocate or Queen's Council, depending on the significance, nature and/or size of the case.

Their lawyer will critique the evidence and may request additional witness statements or a live conference with the chief litigant in order to produce an 'opinion with prospects'. In most cases, for a litigation funder to proceed with a claim, council's opinion must forecast at least a 55% chance of success.

Another determining factor litigation funders will consider is the defendant's ability to pay. If there is any uncertainty, the funder is unlikely to pursue the case because anything can happen in the 18 to 24 months leading up to the trial date. For example, the defendant could be made bankrupt or have their assets liquidated, leaving no recourse to recover funds.

After litigation funders have agreed to pursue the claim, they will hedge their bets by purchasing after-the-event (ATE) insurance. This is an expensive premium that provides cover for payment of the defendant's legal costs, as may be ordered by the court. This is a wise move because in cases where a third party has funded an unsuccessful claim, the funder is held liable for paying the defendant's costs, which is fair as the case was only possible because of the litigation funder's backing.

For example, a litigation funder who provides £300,000 to support a professional negligence claim worth £2.5 million may ask the litigant for £600,000 if they win the case. Additionally, the ATE insurer may request a premium of £50,000 + 10% tax = £55,000, which is to be paid before the trail starts via five monthly instalments of £11,000.

Benefits of Litigation Funding

Litigation funding is a valuable service because it empowers and enables claimants who would otherwise be disenfranchised to seek legal remedy and get justice, especially in professional negligence claims. The funder pays for the litigant's lawyers, barrister and insurance, so they tend to view litigation as a business. Subsequently, a claimant may find themselves under pressure from the litigation funder to negotiate or cut an early deal.

A clever claimant understands they are unlikely to recover 100% of their loss. As a result, if the claimant receives a reasonable offer, litigation funders will try to persuade them to settle early - oftentimes in mediation, because 50% of a significant claim is better than 100% of nothing.

Industry experts know that:

- Most claims never reach a full trial
- The majority of claims are settled in mediation
- Trials can be expensive and result in an unfavourable outcome

As a result, litigation funders, insurers and their lawyers try to protect themselves as much as possible and are more costs-focused and emotionally detached than the average claimant.

For example, when attempting to defend a claim for £5 million they may set a budget of £2 million to settle the case. Before making any offer, their lawyer is likely to exhaust around £250,000 trying to outspend the claimant.

This method is particularly effective if the claimant has no litigation funder because the defendant's lawyers will waste as much of the opponent's time and money as possible by making lots of superfluous interim applications for court orders.

Sometimes, the defendant's lawyers apply to the court seeking for the claimant to provide security for costs. This is evidence that if ordered to, the claimant has the resources to pay the defendant's legal expenses. For example, a lawyer who is confident of defeating the claim and suspects the claimant is running low on cash will make an application to the court and say:

'Defending this vexatious and unmeritorious claim will cost my client around £250,000, even though, on the evidence made available, the claimant is likely to lose at trial, and may have no money to pay our costs either now or in the future.

'Subsequently, we're asking for either the case to be struck out or the claimant to place a significant portion of our estimated defence costs into court.'

In most cases, if the arguments put forward by the defendant's lawyer are persuasive, the court will rule in their favour and may order the claimant to introduce suitable security (cash, property or other assets) into the proceedings for the benefit of the defendant to meet the trial's costs in the event the claim or any part of it is unsuccessful.

MORATORIUM

A moratorium is a statutory insolvency procedure that shields a company from its creditors for a minimum of 20 business days. During this period, pre-moratorium debts do not have to be paid and the company receives considerable protection from:

- Landlords
- Legal actions
- Insolvency proceedings

Current liabilities such as rent, loans and wages must be paid for during the moratorium, and the company will be prohibited from:

- Granting securities
- Obtaining credit of more than £500

The company's director(s) must appoint an insolvency practitioner/monitor to oversee day-to-day operations. This should provide director(s) with enough time to:

- Remodel the business
- Secure additional investment

There are two ways a director can place a company into a moratorium:

1) The in-court process, which involves making an application to the court. The moratorium commences as soon as a court order is made.

2) The out-of-court process, which starts when the relevant documents have

been filed at court. This process is similar to appointing an administrator. But, unlike the administration procedure, directors don't have to notify floating charge holders beforehand.

The necessary documents that must be filed at the court for either process are identical, and include statements from the:

- Director(s) confirming the company either cannot or will soon be unable to pay its debts
- Monitor(s) confirming that a moratorium would help to rescue the company If a winding-up petition has been issued against the company, a moratorium order will only be granted if the court decides this is the best option for creditors. In these circumstances, the court may also make an order for the company to be:

- Wound up
- Placed into administration or another statutory insolvency procedure

If necessary, the company director(s) may seek to extend the duration of the moratorium for:

- Another 20 business days without consent
- Longer than 20 days with the consent of either the court or pre-moratorium creditors.

A monitor may terminate the moratorium prematurely if they decide the company can no longer be rescued. Furthermore, monitors must inform Companies House and all creditors that a moratorium is in place. As a result, it is likely that suppliers will stop offering goods and services on credit.

Although creditors may not commence another statutory insolvency procedure during the moratorium, an astute director will use the time granted by the moratorium period to prepare a proposal that will place their company into either:

1) Administration

2) Company voluntary arrangement (CVA)

Both procedures offer excellent restructuring opportunities, depending on the director(s)' objective. Alternatively, directors can use a creditors' voluntary liquidation (CVL) to wind up a failing company.

Insolvency issues can be complex. Although lawyers are useful, ultimately they will refer you to an insolvency practitioner who has a duty to protect the company's creditors, which sometimes creates a conflict of interest for directors. To avoid this happening, shrewd directors seek support from independent professionals who will:

- Develop a strategy to restructure the business
- Provide impartial advice on statutory and alternative procedures
- Work alongside the insolvency practitioner
- Ensure the insolvency practitioner charges reasonable fees

EPILOGUE

While the insolvency legislation that has been introduced over the past 30 years clearly helped to encourage British enterprise and innovation, in many ways the concerns and rights of creditors have been overlooked.

My company, Insolvency & Law, works closely with creditors to disrupt insolvency proceedings by replacing director-nominated insolvency practitioners with insolvency practitioners chosen by creditors. This may sound like a radical strategy, but usually it is the only way for creditors to gain any real control, which is an absolute travesty because insolvency legislation was originally introduced to protect their interests. Sadly, that doesn't always happen.

In the real world, a perceived conflict of interest exists whenever a company director engages an insolvency practitioner to facilitate an insolvency procedure. How can the insolvency practitioner prioritise creditors' interests over those of the director who is giving them the job? This perception issue is most pressing and needs to be swiftly addressed, especially when you consider that creditors effectively pay for insolvencies.

The number of indolent and expensive insolvency practitioners will reduce rapidly when creditors start viewing insolvency practitioners as employees rather than independent facilitators and realise that creditor-appointed insolvency practitioners tend to:

- Charge lower fees
- Offer higher rates of return
- Be more likely to investigate director(s) without fear or favour

Creditors really have no idea just how much they can increase their power and leverage by uniting and communicating with each other in the weeks, days and hours before they are asked to approve an insolvency practitioner's proposal.

Very little has been done to either protect or extend creditors' rights over the past 30 years. In fact, the Insolvency Rules for England and Wales that came into force in 2016 appear to further alienate and disenfranchise creditors from the insolvency process. Following the introduction of the 2016 rules, unless creditors specifically ask for a meeting they are deemed to have automatically accepted the insolvency practitioner's proposal.

Furthermore, if they want a physical meeting to take place, 10 creditors, 10% of creditors in number or 10% of creditors by value must make a formal request as insolvency practitioners are now expected to communicate virtually via conference or video calls.

The new rules dissuade creditors from engaging with the insolvency process, which only reduces their power to influence proceedings and leaves greater scope for insolvency practitioners and directors to do as they please.

Personally, I am not a fan of the 2016 rules because their introduction forced Insolvency & Law to adjust its business model to ensure that creditors' interests remain a priority, which appears to be a unique position to take.

Depending on the insolvency procedure, creditors have between seven and 14 days to organise and galvanize themselves for a creditors' meeting, which is nowhere near enough time. Subsequently, the first thing creditors must do is make contact with other creditors as quickly as possible. (Ask for the list of all the creditors associated with the insolvency as this can be made available to you upon request.)

I strongly believe insolvency practitioners nominated by directors should serve only in the interim and that creditors should be given 21 to 28 days to communicate and canvas each other's opinions so they can collectively decide to either accept the interim insolvency practitioner or appoint their own.

Having read and heard exactly what the insolvency practitioner plans to do, creditors must tackle their second most important issue - setting the insolvency practitioner fees. This is essential because as a creditor, if you fail to engage in the insolvency process, you will be deemed to have accepted whatever terms, conditions and fees the insolvency practitioner has set for themselves.

It is also important to remember the revenue used to reimburse creditors and pay the insolvency practitioner's fees comes from the insolvency estate. But because insolvency practitioners recover their fees long before creditors are paid out, the more money the insolvency practitioner earns, the less there is for creditors to receive.

Personally, the biggest change I would like to see introduced into corporate insolvency is for the insolvency practitioner's remuneration to be based on a fixed percentage of the assets they realise. In most cases, insolvency practitioners are paid on a time-cost basis, which I think is wrong because it is so easy for them to bill 15 hours for a job that could have been done in 10 hours.

Similarly, if a company enters insolvency with £1 million worth of assets, an insolvency practitioner using the time-cost model can facilitate the procedure over a period of years and run up heading towards £1 million worth of fees.

Whereas the time-cost model literally cannibalises all the proceeds due for realisation, I believe an insolvency practitioner who agrees to share 50% of realisations with creditors will work harder, more efficiently and do more thorough investigations to realise as many assets as possible for maximum values.

Naturally, the idea of an insolvency practitioner sharing 50% of their realisations is unpopular among insolvency practitioners, but it does guarantee creditors receive something when a company enters insolvency, and in many instances the percentages result in greater returns than those achieved using the time-cost model.

A proactive creditor who wants to gain any form of control must obtain the support of other creditors and join the creditors' committee, so if dissatisfied they can simply replace the insolvency practitioner and set their terms, conditions and remuneration in accordance with creditors' desires.

The man who designed the first piece of insolvency legislation, Sir Kenneth Cork, was an accountant, so unsurprisingly you will find that many of the first or oldest insolvency practitioners came from the accounting profession. Similarly, a quick glance at the names and professions of the individuals heading the organisation responsible for amendments to current legislation, The Insolvency Rules Committee, will reveal a list consisting of esteemed accountants, lawyers and judges, but no representative for creditors.

In my opinion, this is the fundamental challenge facing all those seeking to reform the insolvency regime; the legislation is always written by insolvency professionals while groups representing creditors' interests are rarely represented, if at all. An obvious consequence of this oversight is that, generally speaking, creditors do not fare well in insolvencies.